50 Gourmet Desserts for Home

By: Kelly Johnson

Table of Contents

- Dark Chocolate Soufflé
- Classic Tiramisu
- Lemon Lavender Panna Cotta
- Raspberry Macarons
- Vanilla Bean Crème Brûlée
- Hazelnut Chocolate Tart
- Pistachio Gelato
- Salted Caramel Cheesecake
- Lemon Meringue Pie
- Blueberry and Almond Clafoutis
- Flourless Chocolate Cake
- Matcha Green Tea Cheesecake
- Earl Grey Infused Madeleines
- Passionfruit Sorbet
- Red Velvet Cupcakes with Cream Cheese Frosting
- Chocolate Lava Cake
- Coffee-Infused Ice Cream
- Strawberry Basil Sorbet
- Raspberry Mille-Feuille
- Caramelized Apple Tart
- Mango Coconut Panna Cotta
- Chocolate Dipped Churros
- Apricot Pistachio Baklava
- Almond Joy Cheesecake
- Vanilla and Honey Poached Pears
- Fig and Mascarpone Tart
- Dark Chocolate Raspberry Truffles
- Honey Almond Biscotti
- Lemon Blueberry Cheesecake Bars
- Vanilla Bean Rice Pudding
- Coconut Cream Pie
- Saffron and Rosewater Poached Pears
- Espresso Panna Cotta
- Peaches and Cream Tart
- Cherry Clafoutis with Almonds

- Caramel Banana Bread Pudding
- Chocolate Hazelnut Torte
- Pomegranate Sorbet
- Vanilla Bean Ice Cream with Raspberry Coulis
- Saffron and Cardamom Rice Pudding
- White Chocolate Pistachio Bark
- Chocolate Raspberry Eclairs
- Champagne Sorbet
- Pistachio and Rose Water Baklava
- Orange Almond Cake
- Dark Chocolate and Sea Salt Tart
- Lemon and Thyme Olive Oil Cake
- Matcha Chia Pudding
- Cinnamon Sugar Churros with Chocolate Sauce
- Cherry Almond Galette

Dark Chocolate Soufflé

Ingredients:

- 6 ounces dark chocolate (70% cocoa)
- 3 tablespoons unsalted butter
- 1/2 cup milk
- 1/4 cup sugar
- 4 large eggs, separated
- 1 teaspoon vanilla extract
- Pinch of salt
- 1/4 teaspoon cream of tartar
- Powdered sugar (for dusting)

Instructions:

1. **Preheat the Oven**
   Preheat the oven to 375°F (190°C). Butter and sugar the soufflé dishes.
2. **Melt Chocolate**
   In a saucepan, melt the dark chocolate and butter over low heat, stirring constantly. Add the milk and sugar, and stir until smooth.
3. **Separate the Eggs**
   Separate the eggs, placing the whites in a clean bowl and the yolks in another.
4. **Combine with Egg Yolks**
   Whisk the egg yolks and vanilla extract into the melted chocolate mixture.
5. **Whip Egg Whites**
   In a separate bowl, beat the egg whites with a pinch of salt and cream of tartar until stiff peaks form.
6. **Fold Together**
   Gently fold the whipped egg whites into the chocolate mixture in batches.
7. **Bake**
   Spoon the mixture into the prepared soufflé dishes and bake for 18-20 minutes, or until puffed and golden.
8. **Serve**
   Dust with powdered sugar and serve immediately.

Classic Tiramisu

Ingredients:

- 1 1/2 cups heavy cream
- 1/2 cup mascarpone cheese
- 1/4 cup sugar
- 2 teaspoons vanilla extract
- 2 cups strong brewed coffee, cooled
- 2 tablespoons coffee liqueur (optional)
- 1 package ladyfingers
- Cocoa powder (for dusting)

Instructions:

1. **Whip Cream**
   In a large bowl, beat the heavy cream, mascarpone, sugar, and vanilla extract until stiff peaks form.
2. **Prepare the Coffee Mixture**
   Combine the brewed coffee and coffee liqueur in a shallow dish.
3. **Layer the Tiramisu**
   Dip the ladyfingers into the coffee mixture, then layer them in the bottom of a 9x9-inch dish.
4. **Add Cream Layer**
   Spread half of the mascarpone cream over the ladyfingers. Repeat with another layer of dipped ladyfingers and the remaining cream.
5. **Chill**
   Cover and refrigerate for at least 4 hours, or overnight.
6. **Serve**
   Dust with cocoa powder before serving.

Lemon Lavender Panna Cotta

Ingredients:

- 2 cups heavy cream
- 1 cup whole milk
- 1/2 cup sugar
- 1 teaspoon dried lavender flowers
- 1 tablespoon lemon zest
- 1 teaspoon vanilla extract
- 2 teaspoons gelatin powder
- 2 tablespoons cold water

Instructions:

1. **Infuse the Cream**
   In a saucepan, heat the heavy cream, milk, sugar, lavender, and lemon zest over medium heat. Stir until sugar dissolves, then remove from heat and let steep for 10 minutes.
2. **Dissolve Gelatin**
   In a small bowl, sprinkle the gelatin over cold water and let it bloom for 5 minutes. Add it to the warm cream mixture and stir until dissolved.
3. **Add Vanilla**
   Stir in vanilla extract, then strain the mixture to remove the lavender.
4. **Pour into Molds**
   Pour the mixture into individual molds or glasses.
5. **Chill**
   Refrigerate for at least 4 hours or until set.
6. **Serve**
   Serve chilled, garnished with additional lemon zest or lavender.

Raspberry Macarons

Ingredients:

- 1 1/2 cups powdered sugar
- 1 cup almond flour
- 3 large egg whites
- 1/4 cup granulated sugar
- 1/2 teaspoon vanilla extract
- 1/2 cup raspberry jam

Instructions:

1. **Prepare the Dry Ingredients**
   Sift together powdered sugar and almond flour into a large bowl.
2. **Whip Egg Whites**
   In a separate bowl, beat egg whites until soft peaks form. Gradually add granulated sugar and continue beating until stiff peaks form.
3. **Fold Together**
   Gently fold the dry ingredients into the egg whites, being careful not to deflate the mixture.
4. **Pipe the Macarons**
   Transfer the batter to a piping bag and pipe small circles onto a baking sheet lined with parchment paper.
5. **Rest the Macarons**
   Let the piped macarons sit for 30-60 minutes, until they form a skin and no longer stick to your finger.
6. **Bake**
   Preheat the oven to 300°F (150°C). Bake the macarons for 12-15 minutes.
7. **Assemble**
   Once cooled, pair the macarons with raspberry jam to form sandwiches.

Vanilla Bean Crème Brûlée

Ingredients:

- 2 cups heavy cream
- 1 vanilla bean, split and scraped
- 5 large egg yolks
- 1/2 cup sugar
- 1/4 cup light brown sugar (for caramelizing)

Instructions:

1. **Preheat the Oven**
   Preheat the oven to 325°F (163°C). Place 4-6 ramekins in a baking dish.
2. **Infuse the Cream**
   In a saucepan, heat the heavy cream and vanilla bean seeds (scraped from the pod) over medium heat until simmering. Remove from heat and let steep for 10 minutes.
3. **Whisk the Eggs**
   In a separate bowl, whisk together egg yolks and sugar until smooth.
4. **Temper the Eggs**
   Gradually pour the warm cream mixture into the egg mixture while whisking constantly to avoid curdling.
5. **Bake**
   Pour the custard into the ramekins. Fill the baking dish with hot water, about halfway up the sides of the ramekins. Bake for 40-45 minutes, or until set.
6. **Caramelize the Top**
   Let the crème brûlées cool, then sprinkle a thin layer of light brown sugar on top. Use a kitchen torch to caramelize the sugar until golden and crisp.

Hazelnut Chocolate Tart

Ingredients:

- 1 1/4 cups graham cracker crumbs
- 1/4 cup sugar
- 1/4 cup unsalted butter, melted
- 1 1/2 cups dark chocolate chips
- 1/2 cup heavy cream
- 1/2 cup roasted hazelnuts, chopped

Instructions:

1. **Make the Crust**
   Mix graham cracker crumbs, sugar, and melted butter. Press the mixture into the bottom of a tart pan and bake at 350°F (175°C) for 10 minutes.
2. **Make the Filling**
   In a saucepan, heat the heavy cream until simmering. Pour over the chocolate chips and stir until smooth.
3. **Assemble**
   Pour the chocolate mixture into the cooled crust. Sprinkle with chopped hazelnuts.
4. **Chill**
   Refrigerate for 2-3 hours or until set.

Pistachio Gelato

Ingredients:

- 1 1/2 cups shelled pistachios
- 2 cups whole milk
- 1 cup heavy cream
- 3/4 cup sugar
- 4 large egg yolks
- 1 teaspoon vanilla extract

Instructions:

1. **Blend the Pistachios**
   Blend the pistachios in a food processor until finely ground.
2. **Heat the Milk and Cream**
   In a saucepan, heat the milk, cream, and half of the sugar until simmering.
3. **Whisk the Eggs**
   Whisk the egg yolks and remaining sugar in a separate bowl until thick.
4. **Temper the Eggs**
   Slowly pour the hot milk mixture into the eggs, whisking constantly.
5. **Cook the Mixture**
   Return the mixture to the saucepan and cook over low heat until thickened. Stir in the pistachio paste and vanilla extract.
6. **Chill and Freeze**
   Chill the mixture for several hours, then churn in an ice cream maker according to the manufacturer's instructions.

Salted Caramel Cheesecake

Ingredients:

- 1 1/2 cups graham cracker crumbs
- 1/4 cup butter, melted
- 3 packages (8 oz each) cream cheese, softened
- 1 cup sugar
- 3 large eggs
- 1 cup heavy cream
- 1/2 cup salted caramel sauce

Instructions:

1. **Make the Crust**
   Combine graham cracker crumbs and melted butter. Press into the bottom of a springform pan. Bake at 350°F (175°C) for 10 minutes.
2. **Make the Cheesecake Filling**
   Beat the cream cheese and sugar until smooth. Add eggs, one at a time, and mix well.
3. **Bake**
   Pour the filling into the crust and bake at 325°F (163°C) for 45-50 minutes until set.
4. **Cool and Serve**
   Chill the cheesecake for several hours, then top with salted caramel sauce before serving.

Lemon Meringue Pie

Ingredients:

- 1 pre-baked pie crust
- 1 cup granulated sugar
- 2 tablespoons cornstarch
- 1/4 teaspoon salt
- 1 1/2 cups water
- 3 large egg yolks
- 2 tablespoons unsalted butter
- 1/2 cup fresh lemon juice
- Zest of 1 lemon
- 1/4 teaspoon cream of tartar
- 3 large egg whites
- 1/4 cup granulated sugar

Instructions:

1. **Prepare Lemon Filling**
   In a medium saucepan, whisk together sugar, cornstarch, and salt. Add water and cook over medium heat, stirring constantly until the mixture thickens and comes to a boil.
2. **Temper the Egg Yolks**
   In a separate bowl, beat the egg yolks. Gradually add some of the hot mixture into the yolks, whisking constantly to temper them. Pour the egg mixture back into the saucepan and cook for 2 more minutes.
3. **Finish the Filling**
   Remove from heat and stir in butter, lemon juice, and zest. Pour the mixture into the pre-baked pie crust.
4. **Make the Meringue**
   In a clean bowl, beat the egg whites with cream of tartar until soft peaks form. Gradually add sugar and continue beating until stiff peaks form.
5. **Top the Pie**
   Spread the meringue over the lemon filling, ensuring it touches the crust to prevent shrinking.
6. **Bake**
   Bake at 350°F (175°C) for 10-15 minutes until the meringue is golden brown.
7. **Cool and Serve**
   Let the pie cool completely before serving.

Blueberry and Almond Clafoutis

Ingredients:

- 2 cups fresh blueberries
- 1/2 cup sugar
- 3 large eggs
- 1 cup whole milk
- 1/2 cup all-purpose flour
- 1/4 teaspoon almond extract
- 1/4 teaspoon vanilla extract
- 1/4 teaspoon salt
- 1/4 cup sliced almonds

Instructions:

1. **Preheat Oven**
   Preheat the oven to 350°F (175°C). Grease a baking dish and spread the blueberries evenly in the dish.
2. **Make the Batter**
   In a bowl, whisk together eggs, sugar, milk, flour, almond extract, vanilla extract, and salt until smooth.
3. **Pour Over Blueberries**
   Pour the batter over the blueberries and sprinkle with sliced almonds.
4. **Bake**
   Bake for 40-45 minutes, until the clafoutis is set and lightly golden.
5. **Cool and Serve**
   Allow it to cool slightly before serving.

Flourless Chocolate Cake

Ingredients:

- 1 cup semisweet chocolate chips
- 1/2 cup unsalted butter
- 3/4 cup granulated sugar
- 1/4 teaspoon salt
- 3 large eggs
- 1 teaspoon vanilla extract
- 1/2 cup unsweetened cocoa powder

Instructions:

1. **Preheat Oven**
   Preheat the oven to 375°F (190°C). Grease and flour an 8-inch round cake pan.
2. **Melt Chocolate and Butter**
   In a saucepan, melt the chocolate chips and butter over low heat, stirring constantly until smooth.
3. **Mix the Batter**
   Stir the sugar and salt into the melted chocolate. Add eggs, one at a time, followed by the vanilla extract. Stir in the cocoa powder until well combined.
4. **Bake**
   Pour the batter into the prepared pan and bake for 20-25 minutes. The cake should be firm to the touch.
5. **Cool and Serve**
   Allow the cake to cool completely in the pan, then remove and serve.

Matcha Green Tea Cheesecake

Ingredients:

- 1 1/2 cups graham cracker crumbs
- 1/4 cup sugar
- 1/4 cup unsalted butter, melted
- 2 cups cream cheese, softened
- 1 cup sour cream
- 1 cup granulated sugar
- 2 teaspoons matcha powder
- 3 large eggs
- 1 teaspoon vanilla extract

Instructions:

1. **Prepare the Crust**
   Mix graham cracker crumbs, sugar, and melted butter. Press the mixture into the base of a springform pan and bake at 350°F (175°C) for 10 minutes.
2. **Make the Filling**
   In a bowl, beat cream cheese, sour cream, sugar, and matcha powder until smooth. Add eggs one at a time, followed by vanilla extract, and mix until fully combined.
3. **Bake**
   Pour the filling over the crust and bake at 325°F (163°C) for 50-60 minutes, or until set.
4. **Chill and Serve**
   Refrigerate for at least 4 hours before serving.

Earl Grey Infused Madeleines

Ingredients:

- 1 cup all-purpose flour
- 1/2 teaspoon baking powder
- 1/4 teaspoon salt
- 1/2 cup unsalted butter, melted
- 1/2 cup granulated sugar
- 2 large eggs
- 1 teaspoon vanilla extract
- 1 teaspoon Earl Grey tea leaves

Instructions:

1. **Preheat Oven**
   Preheat the oven to 375°F (190°C). Grease a madeleine pan.
2. **Prepare Dry Ingredients**
   In a bowl, sift together flour, baking powder, and salt. Set aside.
3. **Mix the Batter**
   In another bowl, beat together eggs, sugar, and vanilla extract until light and fluffy. Fold in the dry ingredients, then gently fold in the melted butter and Earl Grey tea leaves.
4. **Bake**
   Spoon the batter into the madeleine pan and bake for 10-12 minutes, or until golden.
5. **Serve**
   Allow the madeleines to cool slightly before serving.

Passionfruit Sorbet

Ingredients:

- 1 cup passionfruit pulp (from fresh or frozen fruit)
- 1 cup water
- 3/4 cup sugar
- 1 tablespoon lemon juice

Instructions:

1. **Make the Syrup**
   In a saucepan, combine water and sugar. Heat over medium heat, stirring until sugar dissolves. Remove from heat and let cool.
2. **Prepare the Sorbet Base**
   Stir in the passionfruit pulp and lemon juice into the syrup.
3. **Chill**
   Chill the mixture in the refrigerator for at least 2 hours.
4. **Churn**
   Pour the chilled mixture into an ice cream maker and churn according to the manufacturer's instructions.
5. **Serve**
   Serve immediately or store in the freezer.

Red Velvet Cupcakes with Cream Cheese Frosting

Ingredients:

- 1 1/2 cups all-purpose flour
- 1 cup granulated sugar
- 1 teaspoon baking powder
- 1/2 teaspoon baking soda
- 1/4 teaspoon salt
- 1 teaspoon cocoa powder
- 1/2 cup buttermilk
- 1/4 cup vegetable oil
- 1 large egg
- 1 tablespoon red food coloring
- 1 teaspoon vanilla extract
- 1 teaspoon white vinegar

For Cream Cheese Frosting:

- 8 oz cream cheese, softened
- 1/4 cup unsalted butter, softened
- 2 cups powdered sugar
- 1 teaspoon vanilla extract

Instructions:

1. **Preheat Oven**
   Preheat the oven to 350°F (175°C). Line a muffin tin with cupcake liners.
2. **Mix the Cupcake Batter**
   In a bowl, whisk together flour, sugar, baking powder, baking soda, salt, and cocoa powder. In another bowl, combine buttermilk, oil, egg, food coloring, and vanilla extract. Add the wet ingredients to the dry and mix until smooth.
3. **Bake**
   Divide the batter among the cupcake liners and bake for 18-20 minutes, or until a toothpick comes out clean.
4. **Make the Frosting**
   Beat the cream cheese and butter until smooth. Gradually add powdered sugar and vanilla extract, and beat until fluffy.
5. **Frost and Serve**
   Once the cupcakes are cool, frost with the cream cheese frosting and serve.

Chocolate Lava Cake

Ingredients:

- 6 oz semisweet chocolate
- 1/2 cup unsalted butter
- 1 cup powdered sugar
- 2 large eggs
- 2 egg yolks
- 1/2 teaspoon vanilla extract
- 1/4 cup all-purpose flour

Instructions:

1. **Preheat Oven**
   Preheat the oven to 425°F (220°C). Grease and flour 4 ramekins.
2. **Melt the Chocolate**
   In a saucepan, melt the chocolate and butter over low heat, stirring until smooth.
3. **Make the Batter**
   In a bowl, whisk together powdered sugar, eggs, egg yolks, and vanilla extract. Stir in the melted chocolate and flour until smooth.
4. **Bake**
   Divide the batter among the ramekins and bake for 12-14 minutes, or until the edges are set but the center is still soft.
5. **Serve**
   Let the cakes cool for a minute, then carefully invert onto plates. Serve warm with ice cream or whipped cream.

Coffee-Infused Ice Cream

Ingredients:

- 2 cups heavy cream
- 1 cup whole milk
- 3/4 cup sugar
- 1/2 cup strong brewed coffee (cooled)
- 5 large egg yolks
- 1 teaspoon vanilla extract

Instructions:

1. **Heat the Cream and Milk**
   In a saucepan, heat the cream, milk, and sugar over medium heat, stirring occasionally, until the mixture is warm and sugar is dissolved.
2. **Temper the Eggs**
   In a separate bowl, whisk the egg yolks. Gradually pour the warm cream mixture into the egg yolks while whisking to prevent the eggs from scrambling. Return the mixture to the saucepan and cook over low heat, stirring constantly, until it thickens and coats the back of a spoon.
3. **Add Coffee and Vanilla**
   Remove from heat and stir in the coffee and vanilla extract. Allow the mixture to cool to room temperature, then refrigerate for at least 2 hours.
4. **Churn the Ice Cream**
   Once chilled, pour the mixture into an ice cream maker and churn according to the manufacturer's instructions.
5. **Freeze and Serve**
   Transfer the ice cream to a container and freeze for at least 4 hours before serving.

Strawberry Basil Sorbet

Ingredients:

- 2 cups fresh strawberries, hulled
- 1/2 cup sugar
- 1/2 cup water
- 1/4 cup fresh basil leaves
- 1 tablespoon lemon juice

Instructions:

1. **Prepare the Simple Syrup**
   In a saucepan, combine sugar and water. Heat over medium heat until the sugar dissolves. Remove from heat and add basil leaves. Let steep for 10 minutes, then strain out the basil.
2. **Blend the Strawberries**
   In a blender or food processor, blend the strawberries until smooth. Add the basil syrup and lemon juice, blending again until well combined.
3. **Chill and Freeze**
   Refrigerate the mixture for at least 2 hours. Pour the mixture into an ice cream maker and churn according to the manufacturer's instructions.
4. **Serve**
   Transfer the sorbet to a container and freeze for a few hours before serving.

Raspberry Mille-Feuille

Ingredients:

- 1 package puff pastry sheets
- 1 cup fresh raspberries
- 1 cup whipped cream
- 1/4 cup powdered sugar
- 1 teaspoon vanilla extract
- 1 tablespoon raspberry jam

Instructions:

1. **Prepare the Puff Pastry**
   Preheat the oven to 375°F (190°C). Roll out the puff pastry and cut into 3-inch strips. Place the strips on a baking sheet and bake for 15-20 minutes, or until golden and crisp. Allow to cool.
2. **Make the Filling**
   In a bowl, whip the cream with powdered sugar and vanilla extract until soft peaks form.
3. **Assemble the Mille-Feuille**
   Spread a thin layer of raspberry jam on each puff pastry strip. Top with a dollop of whipped cream and a few fresh raspberries. Stack the layers, alternating between pastry, jam, cream, and berries.
4. **Serve**
   Serve immediately or refrigerate until ready to serve.

Caramelized Apple Tart

Ingredients:

- 1 sheet puff pastry
- 4 medium apples (such as Gala or Granny Smith)
- 1/2 cup granulated sugar
- 2 tablespoons unsalted butter
- 1 teaspoon ground cinnamon
- 1 tablespoon lemon juice

Instructions:

1. **Prepare the Apples**
   Preheat the oven to 375°F (190°C). Peel, core, and slice the apples thinly. Toss with cinnamon and lemon juice.
2. **Prepare the Caramel**
   In a large skillet, melt butter over medium heat. Add sugar and cook until it begins to caramelize. Carefully arrange the apple slices in the skillet, cooking for 5-7 minutes until the apples soften.
3. **Assemble the Tart**
   Unroll the puff pastry onto a baking sheet and arrange the caramelized apples in a pattern on top.
4. **Bake**
   Bake the tart for 20-25 minutes, until the pastry is golden and crisp.
5. **Serve**
   Allow to cool slightly before serving.

Mango Coconut Panna Cotta

Ingredients:

- 1 cup heavy cream
- 1 cup coconut milk
- 1/4 cup sugar
- 2 teaspoons gelatin powder
- 1 ripe mango, peeled and diced
- 1 tablespoon lime juice

Instructions:

1. **Make the Panna Cotta Base**
   In a saucepan, combine heavy cream, coconut milk, and sugar. Heat over low heat until the sugar dissolves and the mixture is warm.
2. **Dissolve the Gelatin**
   Sprinkle gelatin over 2 tablespoons of cold water and let sit for 5 minutes. Stir into the warm cream mixture and whisk until completely dissolved.
3. **Chill**
   Pour the panna cotta mixture into serving glasses and refrigerate for at least 4 hours or until set.
4. **Prepare the Mango Sauce**
   In a blender, puree the mango with lime juice until smooth.
5. **Serve**
   Once the panna cotta is set, top with mango puree and serve.

Chocolate Dipped Churros

Ingredients:

- 1 cup water
- 1/4 cup unsalted butter
- 1 cup all-purpose flour
- 1/4 teaspoon salt
- 2 large eggs
- 1/4 cup granulated sugar
- 1/2 teaspoon cinnamon
- 1/2 cup semisweet chocolate chips
- 1 tablespoon vegetable oil

Instructions:

1. **Make the Churro Dough**
   In a saucepan, combine water and butter. Bring to a boil and stir in the flour and salt. Cook for 2 minutes until the mixture thickens. Remove from heat and allow to cool for 5 minutes. Add the eggs, one at a time, and mix until smooth.
2. **Fry the Churros**
   Heat oil in a deep fryer or large skillet to 375°F (190°C). Pipe the dough into the hot oil in long strips and fry until golden brown, about 3-4 minutes. Remove and drain on paper towels.
3. **Coat with Sugar**
   Mix sugar and cinnamon in a bowl. Roll the churros in the sugar mixture while still warm.
4. **Make the Chocolate Dip**
   Melt the chocolate chips with vegetable oil in a small saucepan over low heat.
5. **Serve**
   Serve churros with warm chocolate dip.

Apricot Pistachio Baklava

Ingredients:

- 1 package phyllo dough
- 1 cup pistachios, chopped
- 1 cup dried apricots, chopped
- 1 cup unsalted butter, melted
- 1/2 cup honey
- 1/2 cup sugar
- 1 teaspoon ground cinnamon

Instructions:

1. **Prepare the Filling**
   In a bowl, combine pistachios, apricots, cinnamon, and sugar.
2. **Assemble the Baklava**
   Brush a baking dish with melted butter. Lay down a sheet of phyllo dough and brush with butter. Repeat with 5-6 layers. Sprinkle a thin layer of filling, then top with 5-6 more layers of phyllo. Repeat until the filling is used.
3. **Cut and Bake**
   Preheat the oven to 350°F (175°C). Cut the baklava into diamond shapes. Bake for 30-35 minutes, or until golden and crisp.
4. **Make the Syrup**
   In a saucepan, combine honey and sugar. Bring to a boil and simmer for 10 minutes.
5. **Finish the Baklava**
   Pour the syrup over the hot baklava and let it soak for at least an hour before serving.

Almond Joy Cheesecake

Ingredients:

- 1 1/2 cups graham cracker crumbs
- 1/4 cup granulated sugar
- 1/2 cup unsalted butter, melted
- 3 cups cream cheese, softened
- 1 cup sugar
- 4 large eggs
- 1 teaspoon vanilla extract
- 1/4 cup unsweetened cocoa powder
- 1/2 cup shredded coconut
- 1/2 cup chopped almonds
- 1/2 cup chocolate chips

Instructions:

1. **Prepare the Crust**
   Mix the graham cracker crumbs, sugar, and melted butter. Press into the base of a springform pan. Bake at 350°F (175°C) for 10 minutes.
2. **Make the Cheesecake Filling**
   In a bowl, beat the cream cheese and sugar until smooth. Add eggs one at a time, followed by vanilla extract. Stir in cocoa powder until well combined.
3. **Add the Mix-ins**
   Fold in shredded coconut and chopped almonds.
4. **Bake**
   Pour the filling over the crust and bake at 325°F (163°C) for 50-60 minutes, or until set.
5. **Serve**
   Allow the cheesecake to cool, then top with chocolate chips before serving.

Vanilla and Honey Poached Pears

Ingredients:

- 4 ripe pears, peeled, cored, and halved
- 1 cup honey
- 2 cups water
- 1 vanilla bean, split and scraped
- 1 cinnamon stick
- 2 whole cloves
- 1 lemon, zested

Instructions:

1. **Prepare the Poaching Liquid**
   In a saucepan, combine honey, water, vanilla bean and seeds, cinnamon stick, cloves, and lemon zest. Bring to a simmer over medium heat, stirring occasionally until the honey dissolves.
2. **Poach the Pears**
   Add the pear halves to the saucepan and reduce the heat to low. Simmer for about 20-25 minutes, or until the pears are tender but not falling apart. Turn the pears occasionally to ensure even cooking.
3. **Serve**
   Remove the pears from the poaching liquid. Increase the heat and simmer the liquid until it thickens into a syrup, about 10 minutes. Drizzle the syrup over the pears before serving.

Fig and Mascarpone Tart

Ingredients:

- 1 package tart crust (or homemade dough)
- 1 cup mascarpone cheese
- 1/4 cup heavy cream
- 1/4 cup powdered sugar
- 1 teaspoon vanilla extract
- 10-12 fresh figs, quartered
- Honey for drizzling

Instructions:

1. **Prepare the Tart Shell**
   Preheat the oven to 375°F (190°C). Roll out the tart dough and press it into a tart pan. Bake for 12-15 minutes, or until golden and crisp. Let cool completely.
2. **Make the Filling**
   In a bowl, whisk together mascarpone, heavy cream, powdered sugar, and vanilla extract until smooth.
3. **Assemble the Tart**
   Spread the mascarpone mixture evenly over the cooled tart crust. Arrange the fig quarters on top in a decorative pattern.
4. **Finish and Serve**
   Drizzle with honey and serve chilled or at room temperature.

Dark Chocolate Raspberry Truffles

Ingredients:

- 8 oz dark chocolate (70% cocoa), chopped
- 1/2 cup heavy cream
- 1/2 cup fresh raspberries, mashed
- 1 teaspoon raspberry extract (optional)
- 1/4 cup cocoa powder (for dusting)

Instructions:

1. **Make the Ganache**
   Heat the heavy cream in a saucepan until it begins to simmer. Pour the cream over the chopped chocolate and let sit for 2-3 minutes before stirring until smooth.
2. **Add Raspberries**
   Stir in the mashed raspberries and raspberry extract (if using). Allow the ganache to cool to room temperature, then refrigerate for 1 hour to firm up.
3. **Form the Truffles**
   Once chilled, scoop tablespoon-sized portions of ganache and roll them into balls. Dust with cocoa powder.
4. **Serve**
   Keep truffles refrigerated until ready to serve.

Honey Almond Biscotti

Ingredients:

- 2 cups all-purpose flour
- 1 cup sliced almonds
- 1/2 teaspoon baking powder
- 1/2 teaspoon salt
- 1/2 cup honey
- 2 large eggs
- 1 teaspoon vanilla extract

Instructions:

1. **Prepare the Dough**
   Preheat the oven to 350°F (175°C). In a bowl, mix flour, baking powder, and salt. In another bowl, whisk eggs, honey, and vanilla extract. Combine the wet and dry ingredients, then fold in the almonds.
2. **Shape the Biscotti**
   Divide the dough in half and shape each portion into a log on a lined baking sheet. Bake for 20-25 minutes, or until golden.
3. **Slice and Bake Again**
   Allow the logs to cool for 10 minutes, then slice them diagonally into 1-inch pieces. Arrange the slices back on the baking sheet and bake for another 10-12 minutes until crisp.
4. **Serve**
   Let the biscotti cool completely before serving.

Lemon Blueberry Cheesecake Bars

Ingredients:

- 1 1/2 cups graham cracker crumbs
- 1/4 cup sugar
- 1/2 cup unsalted butter, melted
- 2 cups cream cheese, softened
- 1 cup sugar
- 2 large eggs
- 1 teaspoon vanilla extract
- 1/4 cup lemon juice
- 1 tablespoon lemon zest
- 1 cup fresh blueberries

Instructions:

1. **Prepare the Crust**
   Preheat the oven to 350°F (175°C). In a bowl, mix graham cracker crumbs, sugar, and melted butter. Press into the base of a greased 9x9-inch baking dish. Bake for 8-10 minutes, then set aside.
2. **Make the Cheesecake Filling**
   In a bowl, beat cream cheese and sugar until smooth. Add eggs one at a time, followed by vanilla extract, lemon juice, and zest. Gently fold in blueberries.
3. **Bake the Bars**
   Pour the cheesecake filling over the crust and bake for 35-40 minutes, or until set. Let cool completely before refrigerating for at least 4 hours.
4. **Serve**
   Cut into squares and serve chilled.

Vanilla Bean Rice Pudding

Ingredients:

- 1 cup Arborio rice
- 4 cups whole milk
- 1/2 cup sugar
- 1 vanilla bean, split and scraped
- Pinch of salt
- 1/2 teaspoon vanilla extract

Instructions:

1. **Cook the Rice**
   In a medium saucepan, bring the milk, sugar, vanilla bean (and its seeds), and salt to a simmer. Add the rice and cook over low heat, stirring frequently, for 25-30 minutes, until the rice is tender and the mixture thickens.
2. **Finish the Pudding**
   Remove from heat and stir in vanilla extract. Remove the vanilla bean.
3. **Serve**
   Let the rice pudding cool slightly before serving. Garnish with cinnamon or fresh berries if desired.

Coconut Cream Pie

Ingredients:

- 1 pre-baked pie crust
- 1 can (13.5 oz) coconut milk
- 1 cup whole milk
- 3/4 cup sugar
- 3 tablespoons cornstarch
- 1/4 teaspoon salt
- 3 large egg yolks
- 1 teaspoon vanilla extract
- 1 cup shredded coconut (toasted)
- Whipped cream for topping

Instructions:

1. **Make the Coconut Filling**
   In a saucepan, whisk together coconut milk, whole milk, sugar, cornstarch, and salt. Bring to a simmer, whisking constantly until it thickens. In a separate bowl, whisk egg yolks. Gradually pour the hot milk mixture into the egg yolks, then return to the saucepan and cook for 2-3 minutes until thickened. Remove from heat and stir in vanilla extract and toasted coconut.
2. **Assemble the Pie**
   Pour the coconut filling into the pre-baked pie crust and refrigerate for at least 4 hours until set.
3. **Serve**
   Top with whipped cream before serving.

Saffron and Rosewater Poached Pears

Ingredients:

- 4 ripe pears, peeled, cored, and halved
- 2 cups water
- 1/2 cup sugar
- 1/2 teaspoon saffron threads
- 1 tablespoon rosewater
- 1 cinnamon stick

Instructions:

1. **Prepare the Poaching Liquid**
   In a saucepan, combine water, sugar, saffron, rosewater, and cinnamon stick. Bring to a simmer until the sugar dissolves.
2. **Poach the Pears**
   Add the pear halves to the saucepan and simmer for 15-20 minutes, or until the pears are tender.
3. **Serve**
   Remove the pears from the liquid. Serve with a drizzle of the poaching syrup.

Espresso Panna Cotta

Ingredients:

- 1 cup heavy cream
- 1/2 cup whole milk
- 1/4 cup sugar
- 1 tablespoon instant espresso powder
- 1 teaspoon vanilla extract
- 1 teaspoon gelatin powder

Instructions:

1. **Dissolve the Gelatin**
   In a small bowl, sprinkle gelatin over 2 tablespoons of cold water and let sit for 5 minutes to bloom.
2. **Make the Panna Cotta Base**
   In a saucepan, combine heavy cream, milk, sugar, and espresso powder. Heat over medium heat until the sugar dissolves and the mixture is hot but not boiling.
3. **Add the Gelatin**
   Stir the bloomed gelatin into the hot cream mixture until dissolved.
4. **Chill**
   Pour the mixture into serving glasses and refrigerate for at least 4 hours or until set.
5. **Serve**
   Top with whipped cream or chocolate shavings before serving.

Peaches and Cream Tart

Ingredients:

- 1 tart crust (store-bought or homemade)
- 3 ripe peaches, peeled and sliced
- 1 cup heavy cream
- 1/4 cup powdered sugar
- 1 teaspoon vanilla extract
- 1/2 cup mascarpone cheese

Instructions:

1. **Prepare the Cream Filling**
   In a mixing bowl, whip the heavy cream with powdered sugar and vanilla extract until stiff peaks form. In another bowl, combine mascarpone cheese with a spoonful of whipped cream to lighten it, then fold in the rest of the whipped cream.
2. **Assemble the Tart**
   Spread the mascarpone cream mixture into the cooled tart crust. Arrange the peach slices artfully on top.
3. **Serve**
   Chill the tart for 2-3 hours before serving.

Cherry Clafoutis with Almonds

Ingredients:

- 1 1/2 cups fresh cherries, pitted
- 1/2 cup all-purpose flour
- 1/4 cup almond meal
- 1/2 cup sugar
- 3 large eggs
- 1 1/2 cups whole milk
- 1 teaspoon vanilla extract
- 1/4 teaspoon almond extract
- Powdered sugar for dusting

Instructions:

1. **Prepare the Batter**
   Preheat the oven to 350°F (175°C). In a mixing bowl, whisk together flour, almond meal, sugar, eggs, milk, and extracts until smooth.
2. **Arrange the Cherries**
   Grease a tart or pie dish and arrange the cherries in a single layer at the bottom.
3. **Pour the Batter**
   Pour the batter over the cherries and bake for 35-40 minutes, or until golden and set in the center.
4. **Serve**
   Dust with powdered sugar before serving. Serve warm or at room temperature.

Caramel Banana Bread Pudding

Ingredients:

- 4 ripe bananas, sliced
- 4 cups cubed stale bread
- 1 1/2 cups heavy cream
- 1/2 cup whole milk
- 3/4 cup brown sugar
- 3 large eggs
- 1 teaspoon vanilla extract
- 1/4 teaspoon cinnamon

Instructions:

1. **Prepare the Bread Pudding**
   Preheat the oven to 350°F (175°C). Grease a baking dish and layer the bread cubes and banana slices in the dish.
2. **Make the Custard**
   In a bowl, whisk together heavy cream, milk, brown sugar, eggs, vanilla, and cinnamon. Pour the custard mixture over the bread and bananas. Let it sit for 15 minutes to soak.
3. **Bake**
   Bake for 45-50 minutes, or until the pudding is set and golden.
4. **Serve**
   Serve warm, optionally drizzled with caramel sauce.

Chocolate Hazelnut Torte

Ingredients:

- 1 cup dark chocolate (70% cocoa)
- 1/2 cup butter
- 3/4 cup sugar
- 1/2 cup ground hazelnuts
- 4 large eggs
- 1/4 teaspoon salt
- 1 teaspoon vanilla extract

Instructions:

1. **Melt the Chocolate**
   Preheat the oven to 350°F (175°C). Grease and line a 9-inch round cake pan. Melt the chocolate and butter together in a heatproof bowl over simmering water.
2. **Make the Batter**
   Whisk the sugar, eggs, ground hazelnuts, salt, and vanilla into the melted chocolate mixture until smooth.
3. **Bake**
   Pour the batter into the prepared pan and bake for 20-25 minutes, or until the center is just set.
4. **Serve**
   Allow the torte to cool completely before serving. Optionally dust with powdered sugar.

Pomegranate Sorbet

Ingredients:

- 2 cups pomegranate juice
- 1/2 cup sugar
- 1 tablespoon lemon juice

Instructions:

1. **Make the Syrup**
   In a saucepan, combine pomegranate juice and sugar. Heat over medium heat, stirring until the sugar dissolves.
2. **Cool and Churn**
   Let the syrup cool to room temperature. Add lemon juice, then pour the mixture into an ice cream maker and churn according to the manufacturer's instructions.
3. **Serve**
   Transfer to a container and freeze for at least 4 hours before serving.

Vanilla Bean Ice Cream with Raspberry Coulis

Ingredients:

- 1 vanilla bean, split and scraped
- 2 cups heavy cream
- 1 cup whole milk
- 3/4 cup sugar
- 1 teaspoon vanilla extract
- 2 cups fresh raspberries
- 1/4 cup sugar (for coulis)

Instructions:

1. **Make the Ice Cream Base**
   In a saucepan, heat the cream, milk, sugar, and vanilla bean (with its seeds) over medium heat. Once the mixture is hot, remove from heat and steep for 30 minutes. Remove the vanilla bean and add vanilla extract.
2. **Churn the Ice Cream**
   Cool the mixture in the fridge for at least 2 hours, then churn in an ice cream maker according to the manufacturer's instructions.
3. **Make the Coulis**
   In a blender, puree the raspberries with sugar. Strain through a fine mesh sieve to remove seeds.
4. **Serve**
   Scoop the ice cream into bowls and drizzle with raspberry coulis.

Saffron and Cardamom Rice Pudding

Ingredients:

- 1/2 cup Arborio rice
- 3 cups whole milk
- 1/2 cup sugar
- 1/4 teaspoon saffron threads
- 4 cardamom pods, crushed
- 1 teaspoon vanilla extract
- 1/4 cup chopped pistachios (optional)

Instructions:

1. **Prepare the Pudding**
   In a saucepan, combine milk, sugar, saffron, and crushed cardamom. Bring to a simmer over medium heat, then stir in the rice.
2. **Cook the Rice**
   Simmer the rice mixture, stirring occasionally, for 30-35 minutes, or until the rice is tender and the mixture thickens.
3. **Finish**
   Stir in vanilla extract and let the pudding cool slightly.
4. **Serve**
   Garnish with chopped pistachios before serving.

White Chocolate Pistachio Bark

Ingredients:

- 8 oz white chocolate, chopped
- 1/2 cup shelled pistachios, chopped
- 1/4 teaspoon sea salt

Instructions:

1. **Melt the Chocolate**
   Melt the white chocolate in a heatproof bowl over simmering water.
2. **Assemble the Bark**
   Line a baking sheet with parchment paper. Pour the melted chocolate onto the sheet and spread into a thin layer. Sprinkle with chopped pistachios and sea salt.
3. **Set the Bark**
   Refrigerate for 1-2 hours, or until set.
4. **Serve**
   Break into pieces and serve.

Chocolate Raspberry Eclairs

Ingredients:

- 1 batch choux pastry (recipe below)
- 1 cup heavy cream
- 1/4 cup powdered sugar
- 1 teaspoon vanilla extract
- 1/2 cup raspberry jam
- 4 oz dark chocolate (for glazing)

Choux Pastry:

- 1/2 cup water
- 1/2 cup unsalted butter
- 1 cup all-purpose flour
- 1/4 teaspoon salt
- 4 large eggs

Instructions:

1. **Make the Choux Pastry**
   Preheat the oven to 400°F (200°C). In a saucepan, melt the butter in water over medium heat. Stir in the flour and salt, then cook for 2 minutes. Remove from heat and whisk in eggs one at a time until smooth.
2. **Shape and Bake the Eclairs**
   Pipe the choux dough onto a lined baking sheet into 4-inch logs. Bake for 25-30 minutes until puffed and golden. Let cool.
3. **Prepare the Filling**
   Whisk together the cream, powdered sugar, and vanilla extract until stiff peaks form. Fill each éclair with whipped cream and a spoonful of raspberry jam.
4. **Glaze the Eclairs**
   Melt the dark chocolate in a heatproof bowl over simmering water. Dip the tops of each éclair into the melted chocolate.
5. **Serve**
   Let the glaze set before serving.

Champagne Sorbet

Ingredients:

- 1 cup champagne or sparkling wine
- 1/2 cup water
- 1/2 cup sugar
- 1 tablespoon lemon juice

Instructions:

1. **Prepare the Syrup**
   In a saucepan, combine water and sugar. Heat over medium heat until the sugar dissolves, then remove from heat. Stir in the champagne and lemon juice.
2. **Freeze the Sorbet**
   Pour the mixture into an ice cream maker and churn according to the manufacturer's instructions. If you don't have an ice cream maker, pour the mixture into a shallow dish and freeze, stirring every 30 minutes until the sorbet reaches a slushy consistency.
3. **Serve**
   Scoop the sorbet into bowls or glasses and serve immediately.

Pistachio and Rose Water Baklava

Ingredients:

- 1 package phyllo dough
- 2 cups shelled pistachios, chopped
- 1/2 cup granulated sugar
- 1 teaspoon ground cinnamon
- 1 cup unsalted butter, melted
- 1 cup honey
- 1 tablespoon rose water

Instructions:

1. **Prepare the Filling**
   In a bowl, combine chopped pistachios, sugar, and cinnamon.
2. **Assemble the Baklava**
   Preheat the oven to 350°F (175°C). Brush a baking dish with melted butter and layer 6 sheets of phyllo dough, brushing each layer with butter. Sprinkle a thin layer of pistachio mixture over the dough. Repeat with 6 more sheets of phyllo and more pistachios. Continue layering and filling until all ingredients are used, finishing with 6 layers of phyllo dough on top.
3. **Cut and Bake**
   Cut the baklava into squares or diamonds and bake for 45-50 minutes, until golden and crispy.
4. **Make the Syrup**
   In a saucepan, combine honey and rose water. Heat gently, stirring until smooth, then pour over the hot baklava immediately after baking.
5. **Serve**
   Let the baklava cool to room temperature before serving.

Orange Almond Cake

Ingredients:

- 1 1/2 cups almond flour
- 1/2 cup all-purpose flour
- 1/2 teaspoon baking powder
- 1/4 teaspoon salt
- 1/2 cup unsalted butter, softened
- 1 cup sugar
- 3 large eggs
- Zest of 1 orange
- 1/4 cup fresh orange juice
- 1/2 teaspoon vanilla extract

Instructions:

1. **Prepare the Batter**
   Preheat the oven to 350°F (175°C). Grease and flour an 8-inch round cake pan. In a bowl, whisk together almond flour, all-purpose flour, baking powder, and salt.
2. **Cream the Butter and Sugar**
   In a separate bowl, beat the butter and sugar until light and fluffy. Add eggs one at a time, then stir in orange zest, orange juice, and vanilla extract.
3. **Combine and Bake**
   Gradually fold in the dry ingredients until just combined. Pour the batter into the prepared pan and bake for 30-35 minutes, or until a toothpick inserted comes out clean.
4. **Serve**
   Let the cake cool before removing from the pan and serving.

Dark Chocolate and Sea Salt Tart

Ingredients:

- 1 pre-baked tart crust
- 8 oz dark chocolate (70% cocoa), chopped
- 1/2 cup heavy cream
- 1 tablespoon unsalted butter
- 1/4 teaspoon sea salt

Instructions:

1. **Make the Ganache**
   In a saucepan, heat the heavy cream until it begins to simmer. Remove from heat and pour over the chopped chocolate. Let it sit for 2 minutes, then stir until smooth. Stir in the butter until fully incorporated.
2. **Fill the Tart**
   Pour the ganache into the pre-baked tart crust and smooth the top with a spatula.
3. **Chill and Garnish**
   Refrigerate the tart for at least 2 hours, until the ganache sets. Sprinkle with sea salt before serving.
4. **Serve**
   Slice the tart and enjoy!

Lemon and Thyme Olive Oil Cake

Ingredients:

- 1 1/2 cups all-purpose flour
- 1 teaspoon baking powder
- 1/2 teaspoon salt
- 1/2 cup extra virgin olive oil
- 1 cup sugar
- 3 large eggs
- Zest of 2 lemons
- 2 tablespoons fresh lemon juice
- 2 teaspoons fresh thyme leaves
- 1/2 cup whole milk

Instructions:

1. **Prepare the Batter**
   Preheat the oven to 350°F (175°C). Grease and flour a 9-inch cake pan. In a bowl, whisk together flour, baking powder, and salt.
2. **Mix Wet Ingredients**
   In another bowl, whisk together olive oil, sugar, eggs, lemon zest, lemon juice, and thyme until smooth.
3. **Combine and Bake**
   Gradually add the dry ingredients into the wet ingredients, alternating with milk, until fully combined. Pour the batter into the prepared pan and bake for 35-40 minutes, or until a toothpick comes out clean.
4. **Serve**
   Let the cake cool in the pan for 10 minutes, then remove and serve.

Matcha Chia Pudding

Ingredients:

- 1 tablespoon matcha powder
- 1 cup almond milk
- 2 tablespoons maple syrup
- 1/4 teaspoon vanilla extract
- 3 tablespoons chia seeds

Instructions:

1. **Make the Pudding**
   In a bowl, whisk together matcha powder, almond milk, maple syrup, and vanilla extract until smooth.
2. **Add Chia Seeds**
   Stir in chia seeds and mix well. Let the mixture sit for 5 minutes, then stir again.
3. **Chill**
   Cover and refrigerate for at least 4 hours or overnight, until the pudding thickens.
4. **Serve**
   Serve chilled, topped with fresh fruit or granola.

Cinnamon Sugar Churros with Chocolate Sauce

Ingredients:

- 1 cup water
- 1/4 cup unsalted butter
- 1 tablespoon sugar
- 1/2 teaspoon salt
- 1 cup all-purpose flour
- 2 large eggs
- 1 teaspoon vanilla extract
- 1/4 cup sugar (for coating)
- 1 teaspoon cinnamon (for coating)
- Vegetable oil for frying

Chocolate Sauce:

- 4 oz dark chocolate
- 1/2 cup heavy cream
- 1 tablespoon sugar

Instructions:

1. **Make the Churro Dough**
   In a saucepan, combine water, butter, sugar, and salt. Bring to a boil, then remove from heat. Stir in flour until smooth. Let the mixture cool for 5 minutes, then add eggs and vanilla extract, mixing until combined.
2. **Fry the Churros**
   Heat oil in a deep frying pan over medium-high heat. Fill a piping bag with the churro dough and pipe 4-inch lengths of dough into the hot oil. Fry until golden brown and crisp, about 2-3 minutes per side.
3. **Coat in Cinnamon Sugar**
   Combine sugar and cinnamon in a bowl. Remove the churros from the oil and coat them in the cinnamon sugar mixture.
4. **Make the Chocolate Sauce**
   Heat the cream in a saucepan until it begins to simmer, then pour over the chopped chocolate. Stir until smooth and add sugar to taste.
5. **Serve**
   Serve the churros with chocolate sauce for dipping.

Cherry Almond Galette

Ingredients:

- 1 sheet puff pastry
- 2 cups fresh cherries, pitted
- 1/4 cup sugar
- 1 tablespoon cornstarch
- 1/4 teaspoon almond extract
- 1 egg (for egg wash)
- Sliced almonds (for topping)

Instructions:

1. **Prepare the Filling**
   Preheat the oven to 375°F (190°C). In a bowl, toss cherries with sugar, cornstarch, and almond extract.
2. **Assemble the Galette**
   Roll out the puff pastry on a baking sheet lined with parchment paper. Spoon the cherry mixture into the center, leaving a border around the edges. Fold the edges over the cherries to form a rustic crust.
3. **Bake**
   Brush the edges of the pastry with an egg wash and sprinkle with sliced almonds. Bake for 35-40 minutes, or until the pastry is golden and the filling is bubbling.
4. **Serve**
   Let cool slightly before serving. Enjoy warm or at room temperature.

www.ingramcontent.com/pod-product-compliance
Lightning Source LLC
LaVergne TN
LVHW081338060526
838201LV00055B/2717